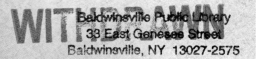
UNDERSTANDING ANXIETY

WHAT ARE PHOBIAS?

THERESE M. SHEA

PowerKiDS press.

NEW YORK

Published in 2021 by The Rosen Publishing Group, Inc.
29 East 21st Street, New York, NY 10010

First Edition

Editor: Kristen Susienka
Book Design: Rachel Rising

Photo Credits: Cover pathdoc/Shutterstock.com; Cover RHJPhtotoandilustration/Shutterstock.com; Cover Toma Stepunina/Shutterstock.com; Cover Syda Productions/Shutterstock.com; Cover, pp. 1,3, 4, 6,8, 10, 11, 12, 14, 16, 18, 20, 22, 23, 24 (background) Flas100/Shutterstock.com; Cover, pp. 1, 3, 5, 7,9,10,11,13,15,17,19,21 (text box) mhatzapa/Shutterstock.com; p. 4 Anatoliy Karlyuk/Shutterstock.com; pp. 5, 17 Photographee.eu/Shutterstock.com; p. 6 ESB Professional/Shutterstock.com; p. 7 Skylines/Shutterstock.com; p. 9 Gregory Johnston/Shutterstock.com; p. 11 camilla$$/Shutterstock.com; p. 12 Vera Larina/Shutterstock.com; p. 13 holwichaikawee/Shutterstock.com; p. 14 photomak/Shutterstock.com; p. 15 fizkes/Shutterstock.com; p. 16 mypokcik/Shutterstock.com; p. 18 naluwan/Shutterstock.com; p. 19 4Max/Shutterstock.com; p. 20 Here/Shutterstock.com; p. 21 Ekaterina Vidyasova/Shutterstock.com; p. 22 pikselstock/Shutterstock.com.

Some of the images in this book illustrate individuals who are models. The depictions do not imply actual situations or events.

Cataloging-in-Publication Data

Names: Shea, Therese M.
Title: What are phobias? / Therese M. Shea.
Description: New York : PowerKids Press, 2021. | Series: Understanding anxiety | Includes glossary and index.
Identifiers: ISBN 9781725317970 (pbk.) | ISBN 9781725317994 (library bound) | ISBN 9781725317987 (6 pack)
Subjects: LCSH: Phobias–Juvenile literature. | Phobias–Treatment–Juvenile literature.
Classification: LCC RC535.S427 2021 | DDC 616.85'225–dc23

Manufactured in the United States of America

CPSIA Compliance Information: Batch #CSPK20. For Further Information contact Rosen Publishing, New York, New York at 1-800-237-9932.

Find us on

CONTENTS

FEAR VS. PHOBIA

We're all afraid of something. That's common. However, sometimes fears are very strong. They make it hard to live normally. This kind of fear is called a phobia.

With a phobia, someone has a higher degree, or amount, of fear about something. The anxiety, or worry, caused by the fear lasts for a long time. Phobias might stop people from going places or being with others. It doesn't matter if someone tells them that their worry doesn't make sense. The phobia is in charge.

PHOBIAS ARE A KIND OF **ANXIETY DISORDER**. PEOPLE WITH ANXIETY DISORDERS FEEL LOTS OF WORRY OR FEAR ABOUT EVERYDAY THINGS.

TYPES OF PHOBIAS

Some doctors place phobias into three groups. One is agoraphobia (ah-guh-ruh-FOH-bee-uh). That means anxiety about being in public places. People with agoraphobia fear getting trapped or embarrassed, or made to feel foolish, in open places with a lot of people. They worry they won't be able to escape or get help.

Another kind of phobia is social anxiety. This is a fear of being with other people in social settings. Those with this phobia worry they'll get embarrassed or be judged badly. They may drop out of school or quit work to avoid people.

The third kind of phobia is a specific phobia. It means having terrible fear about certain objects or **situations**, such as spiders or tight spaces. A person with a specific phobia **avoids** the object or situation, even if it makes life much harder. Just thinking about the phobia might set off anxiety.

While everyone feels fear sometimes, phobias are always with people. If you're afraid to make a speech at school, it doesn't mean you have a phobia. Phobias come with certain strong symptoms, or signs, too.

COMMON CHILDHOOD PHOBIAS

- ANIMALS
- BLOOD
- THE DARK
- FLYING
- GETTING SICK
- HEIGHTS
- BUGS AND SPIDERS
- NEEDLES
- TIGHT SPACES
- A FAMILY MEMBER OR PET GETTING SICK OR HURT

WHAT ARE THE SYMPTOMS?

    A symptom is a change in the body that shows that something's wrong. A runny nose is a symptom of a cold, for example. People with phobias have symptoms, too.

    However, different people show different symptoms, even if they have the same phobia. Some symptoms are physical, which means they happen in the body. Some are psychological (sy-kuh-LAH-jih-kuhl), which means they happen in the mind. Check out the box on the next page to find out more about phobia symptoms.

FOR A PERSON WITH A PHOBIA, JUST THINKING OF THEIR FEARED OBJECT OR SITUATION COULD CAUSE ONE OR MORE OF THESE SYMPTOMS TO HAPPEN.

COMMON SYMPTOMS OF PHOBIAS

PHYSICAL

- SWEATING
- SHAKING
- SHORT, QUICK BREATHS
- HEART BEATING FAST
- FEELING DIZZY OR FAINT
- THROWING UP
- TINGLING IN THE BODY
- CHEST PAINS
- FEELING VERY HOT OR VERY COLD
- FEELING TIRED OR WEAK

PSYCHOLOGICAL

- FEELING LIKE THE BODY AND MIND AREN'T CONNECTED
- UNABLE TO THINK CLEARLY BECAUSE OF WORRY
- FEARING A LOSS OF CONTROL
- PANIC
- FEARING DEATH

CAUSES OF PHOBIAS

The causes of phobias aren't always understood. It's thought that a scary event can start a phobia. However, it's also believed that certain people are more likely to have phobias. Phobias may be learned from family or caused by **genes**. Special **chemicals** in the brain can cause feelings of worry, too.

Most people with phobias **develop** them as children, teenagers, or young adults. Childhood phobias don't last as long as the phobias of older people. Older people's phobias can last for years unless they get help.

ARACHNOPHOBIA
FEAR OF SPIDERS

13

GETTING HELP

A phobia can make it hard for a person to live. For young people, this might mean not playing with friends or losing sleep. If this happens over a long time, a person should get help.

Doctors can help. They'll check the person's physical health. Then, they'll ask questions about the person's thoughts, feelings, and actions. They'll use the answers to find out what kind of phobia the person has and the best way to treat it. They may suggest seeing a special kind of doctor.

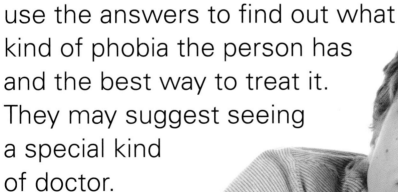

PSYCHIATRISTS AND PSYCHOLOGISTS ARE TWO KINDS OF DOCTORS WHO CAN FIND OUT IF SOMEONE HAS A PHOBIA AND HELP TREAT IT.

15

TREATING A PHOBIA

For some, the best way to treat a phobia is through exposure **therapy**. This means being exposed to, or shown, the object or situation of the phobia a bit at a time. This can help someone learn to **react** to it differently over time.

Sometimes another kind of therapy is used with exposure therapy. It's called cognitive behavioral therapy (CBT), and it just means talking about fears. This can help someone learn to control their feelings so they don't get in the way of their life.

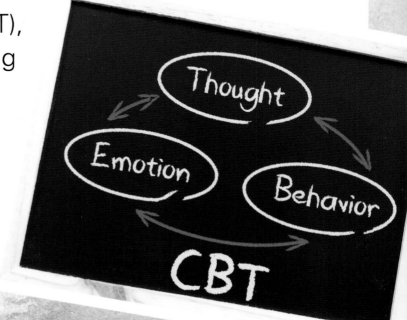

DOCTORS MAY ALSO SUGGEST TAKING MEDICATIONS, OR DRUGS, TO HELP CONTROL A PHOBIA. ONLY DO THIS IF YOUR DOCTOR SAYS TO DO SO.

LIVING WITH A PHOBIA

The goal of treating a phobia is to live better with the phobia. The person with the phobia learns to control their fear and feelings. They can live a normal life and may even lose the fear over time.

There are other things people can do to help lower the worry that goes with phobias. Some of these things are exercising, eating healthier, and getting enough sleep. Learning special ways to breathe during hard situations can help lower the fear, too.

DIFFERENT, QUIETER ACTIVITIES MIGHT HELP PEOPLE. TWO EXAMPLES ARE **YOGA** AND **MEDITATION**.

19

HOW TO HELP OTHERS

Even if you don't have a phobia, you might know someone who does. Millions of Americans have them. Learning more about phobias means you can help those who have them.

It's important to treat people with phobias with respect. Never tell someone they're just being silly or that they should just face their fears. Instead, listen to the person. Talking is one thing that can help. You can also give people **support** as they go for help.

THERE ARE SOME SUPPORT GROUPS FOR THOSE WITH PHOBIAS AND OTHER ANXIETY DISORDERS. PEOPLE IN THESE GROUPS SHARE WHAT THEIR LIVES ARE LIKE AND HOW THEY'VE FOUND HELP.

NOT ALONE

If you do have a phobia—or think you might—you're not alone. Sometimes, the fear can make you feel lonely. You might think you can't live like other people. However, many people are ready to help you.

With help, you can beat your fears. You can live a normal life. You can learn to control your anxiety and its symptoms. Reaching out for help is the most important thing you can do to treat your phobia.

GLOSSARY

anxiety disorder: A disorder marked by fear or stress beyond the usual reaction to something.

avoid: To stay away from something.

chemical: Matter that can be mixed with other matter to cause changes.

develop: To grow and change.

gene: Tiny parts of a cell that are passed from parent to child and that decide features in the child, such as eye color.

meditation: The act of focusing on one's breathing, emotions, and thoughts in a quiet way.

react: To change or behave in a way when something happens.

situation: Facts, conditions, and events that affect someone at a time and place.

support: Being there for others in a time of need with helpful words or actions.

therapy: A way of dealing with problems to make people feel better.

yoga: A kind of exercise for mental and physical health.

INDEX

A

agoraphobia, 6, 7
anxiety, 4, 5, 6, 8, 21, 22
anxiety disorder, 5, 21
arachnophobia, 12

C

cognitive behavioral therapy, 16

D

doctors, 6, 14, 15, 17

E

exposure therapy, 16

F

fear, 4, 5, 6, 8, 16, 18, 20, 22

G

genes, 12

M

medication, 17
meditation, 19

P

panic, 11
psychiatrist, 15
psychologist, 15

S

social anxiety, 6
specific phobia, 8, 9
symptoms, 8, 10, 11, 22

T

therapy, 16
trypanophobia, 9

W

worry, 4, 5, 11, 12, 18

Y

yoga, 19

WEBSITES

Due to the changing nature of Internet links, PowerKids Press has developed an online list of websites related to the subject of this book. This site is updated regularly. Please use this link to access the list: www.powerkidslinks.com/ua/phobias